BIG BAND CLARINET
EASY PLAY SOLOS

Editor: Tony Esposito
Cover Illustration: Joseph Klucar

© 1995 WARNER BROS. PUBLICATIONS
All Rights Reserved

MW00583000

AND THE ANGELS SING

Words by
JOHNNY MERCER

Music by
ZIGGY ELMAN

ALEXANDER'S RAGTIME BAND

Words and Music by
IRVING BERLIN

APRIL IN PARIS

Words by
E.Y. HARBURG

Music by
VERNON DUKE

From the Warner Bros. Motion Picture "CASABLANCA"

AS TIME GOES BY

Words and Music by
HERMAN HUPFELD

Moderately slow

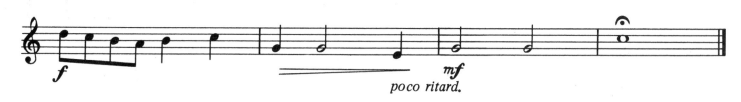

poco ritard.

BEGIN THE BEGUINE

Words and Music by
COLE PORTER

Moderately

7

BODY AND SOUL

Words by
EDWARD HEYMAN, ROBERT SOUR
and FRANK EYTON

Music by
JOHN GREEN

DO NOTHIN' TILL YOU HEAR FROM ME

Lyrics by
BOB RUSSELL

Music by
DUKE ELLINGTON

I GOT RHYTHM

By GEORGE GERSHWIN
and IRA GERSHWIN

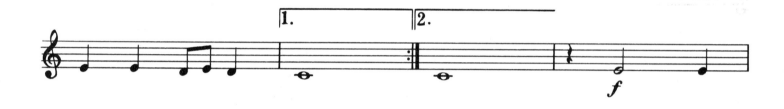

I'LL SEE YOU IN MY DREAMS

Words by
GUS KAHN

Music by
ISHAM JONES

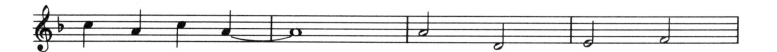

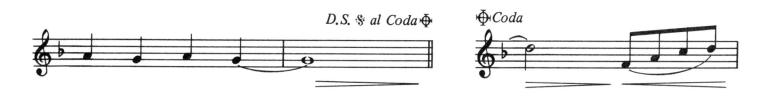

I'M GETTIN' SENTIMENTAL OVER YOU

Words by
NED WASHINGTON

Music by
GEORGE BASSMAN

INDIAN SUMMER

Words by
AL DUBIN

Music by
VICTOR HERBERT

JERSEY BOUNCE

Words by
BUDDY FEYNE

Music by
BOBBY PLATER, TINY BRADSHAW
and EDWARD JOHNSON

JUMPIN' AT THE WOODSIDE

Music by
COUNT BASIE

LOVER, COME BACK TO ME!

Words by
OSCAR HAMMERSTEIN II

Music by
SIGMUND ROMBERG

MOONGLOW

By WILL HUDSON, EDDIE DE LANGE
and IRVING MILLS

NIGHT AND DAY

Words and Music by
COLE PORTER

SATIN DOLL

Words and Music by
JOHNNY MERCER, DUKE ELLINGTON
and BILLY STRAYHORN

Moderately, with a beat

STAR DUST

Words by MITCHELL PARISH

Music by
HOAGY CARMICHAEL

STRIKE UP THE BAND

By GEORGE GERSHWIN
and IRA GERSHWIN

Slow March Tempo

TIME ON MY HANDS
(You in My Arms)

Words by
HAROLD ADAMSON and MACK GORDON

Music by
VINCENT YOUMANS

TUXEDO JUNCTION

Words by
BUDDY FEYNE

Music by
ERSKINE HAWKINS, WILLIAM JOHNSON
and JULIAN DASH